Amy Pell

A New True Book

MARS

By Dennis B. Fradin

CHILDRENS PRESS ®

CHICAGO

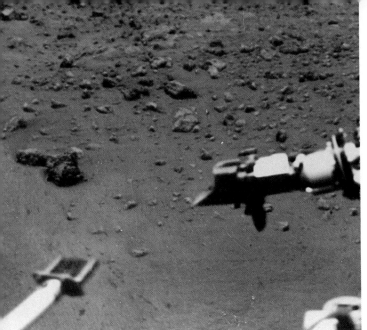

Sampler scoop and arm of the *Viking* probe

For My Friends, Marsha and Rich Newman

PHOTO CREDITS
Art—John Forsberg—6, 7
The Bettmann Archive—10 (both), 13, 14, 19, 20, 23 (right)
Field Museum of Natural History (# A77818C)—10 (top)
NASA—Cover, 2, 4, 8, 9, 29, 36 (both), 39, 41, 42, 44
NASA-JET PROPULSION LAB—27 (left), 28 (both), 30 (both), 33, 35, 45
James Oberg—27 (right)
Wide World Photos, Inc.—23 (left), 25
Yerkes Observatory Photograph—15, 17, 21 (both)
COVER: *Viking* lands on Mars.

Library of Congress Cataloging-in-Publication Data

Fradin, Dennis B.
  Mars / by Dennis B. Fradin.
    p.   cm. — (A New true book)
  Includes index.
  Summary: Examines the planet Mars and investigations both past and future to increase our knowledge of it.
  ISBN 0-516-01164-2
  1. Mars (Planet)—Juvenile literature. [1. Mars (Planet)]
I. Title.
QB641.F72 1989   88-39122
523.4'3—dc19   CIP
                                              AC

TABLE OF CONTENTS

Our Solar System...5

Mars and Ancient People...11

Mars Through the Telescope...14

Bigger and Better Telescopes...21

Exploring Mars by Spacecraft...26

More Questions About Mars...37

People Will Go to Mars!...39

Facts About Mars...46

Words You Should Know...46

Index...47

OUR SOLAR SYSTEM

There are many, many millions of stars in space. There are millions of times as many stars as there are people in the world.

Every star but one looks like a point of light to us. They seem small because they are so far away. The one star that looks big is the Sun. The Sun isn't especially big or bright for

a star. It just looks bigger
and brighter because it is
much closer to Earth.

Nine planets move
around the Sun in orbits
shaped like flattened
circles. Mercury and
Venus are the two planets
closest to the Sun. Earth is

the third planet from the
Sun. The six that are
beyond Earth are Mars,
Jupiter, Saturn, Uranus,
Neptune, and Pluto.

The Sun and its nine
planets are the main
members of the *Solar
System*. The Solar System

can be thought of as the Sun's family. Other major members of this family are the moons—objects that orbit most of the planets.

Moons orbit planets.

Earth as seen from outer space

Life cannot exist on the
Sun because it is too hot.
But we know that life can
exist on planets. All we
need do is look at our own
planet Earth to prove that!

Diorama of the Carnac rock formation where prehistoric people worshiped the Sun (above). Hipparchus, the Greek astronomer (below left), and the Arabian astronomers (below right) studied and made measurements of the heavens.

MARS AND ANCIENT PEOPLE

Ancient people saw five planets in the sky. The five were Mercury, Venus, Mars, Jupiter, and Saturn. The ancient people did not know that Earth also is a planet. Uranus, Neptune and Pluto were not discovered until after telescopes were invented. Telescopes make distant objects look closer.

The word *planet* means "wandering star."

The ancient people did not know much about the planets. They named the planets after gods. For example, the brightest planet was very white and lovely. Many ancient people named it after their goddess of love. Another planet was colored blood-red. Blood reminded people of war. As a result, people named the red planet after their war god.

Engraving of Mars, the Roman god of war.

Most names the ancient Romans gave to the planets are the ones we use today. The Romans named the bright, white planet Venus, for their goddess of love. They named the red planet Mars, after their god of war.

MARS
THROUGH
THE
TELESCOPE

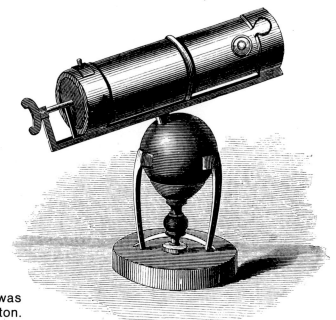

The first reflecting telescope was invented and built by Isaac Newton.

Telescopes were invented in the early 1600s. Astronomers aimed their telescopes at the heavens. They saw no details on the stars because the distance was too great. However, they did see markings on the planets.

They spotted white areas
on the north and south
poles of Mars. Mars also
had greenish-gray regions
that grew larger during
certain seasons.
Astronomers thought ice
and snow caused the
white areas at the poles.

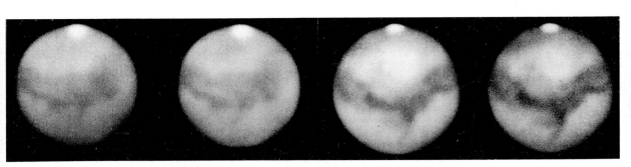

Series of photographs taken of Mars in 1909

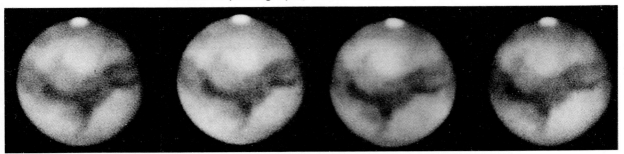

At first they thought the greenish-gray regions were oceans. Later they thought they were plants. They figured that these regions enlarged during Mars' spring and summer because the plants were growing.

Some astronomers decided that if Mars had plants, then it might have animals or even people. In 1784 the great astronomer William Herschel said he

William
Herschel

believed in Martians. He also said that Mars probably was very much like the Earth.

The idea of Martians thrilled the world. Every 16 years, Mars makes its closest approach to the Earth. At those times, people tried to contact the

Martians. In the early 1800s people tried to grow a huge wheat field shaped like a triangle. They thought the Martians would see the field with their telescopes and know that someone had planted it.

In 1877 the Italian astronomer Giovanni Schiaparelli said he had seen channels on Mars. The Italian word for *channels* was wrongly translated into English as the word "canals."

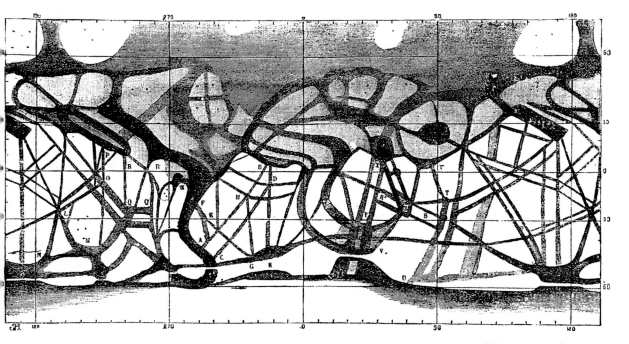

Schiaparelli drew this chart of Mars showing
the double channels he saw through his telescope.

Some English-speaking
astronomers soon claimed
to have seen "canals" on
Mars, too.

A *theory* (idea) about
Mars became popular.
Mars was a dying planet,
this theory said. The

Artists loved to draw pictures of invaders from Mars.
This illustration appeared in *The War of the Worlds*,
written by H. G. Wells.

Martians had built the
canals to bring water to
their crops. Authors wrote
stories about Martians.
Some were about the
Martians invading the Earth
in search of a new home.

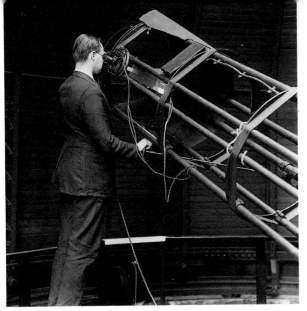

The Yerkes Observatory used the 24-inch Richey reflector telescope (above) about 1930 and the 40-inch reflecting telescope (right) about 1900.

BIGGER AND BETTER TELESCOPES

Several huge telescopes were built in the early 1900s. They gave astronomers a better view of heavenly bodies. The new telescopes showed something surprising about Mars—the canals did not seem to be there! The earlier astronomers had been wrong. Their weaker telescopes had played tricks on their eyes.

Better telescopes helped astronomers learn about Mars. It appeared unlikely that Martians existed. Mars seemed to lack the air needed by advanced life. And the red planet seemed to be too cold.

Orson Welles (above) broadcast "The War of the Worlds" radio show. The illustration (right) of a wounded Martian appeared in the book written by H. G. Wells.

By 1930 most astronomers did not believe in Martians. But the public did. A story about a Martian invasion was on radio in 1938. It was *The War of the Worlds*, by H. G. Wells. Because many

23

people turned on their radios in the middle of the show, they did not know it was just a story. Thinking Martians had landed, hundreds of people fled their homes!

In the 1950s, many people claimed that they saw *flying saucers*, or *UFO's* (*unidentified flying objects*). The flying saucers supposedly were spaceships from other worlds. Many people thought they had Martians aboard.

No proof has ever been found that flying saucers exist. Few scientists believe in them. Yet even today some people believe in flying saucers. And occasionally people still claim to have seen "men from Mars."

EXPLORING MARS BY SPACECRAFT

The space age began in 1957, when the Soviet Union (USSR) launched *Sputnik I*, the first artificial satellite to orbit Earth.

Soon the USSR and the United States were launching many rockets into space. Both nations made plans to send unmanned *space probes*

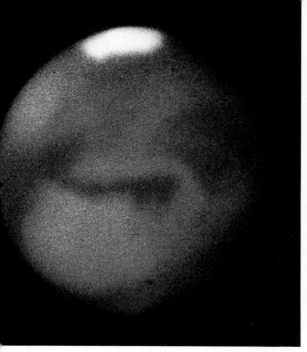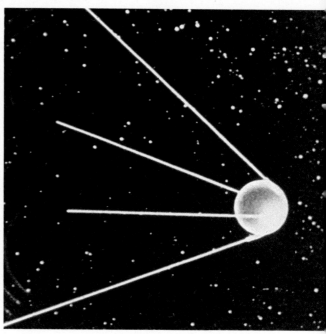

Ground-based telescope photograph of Mars taken by Dr. Robert Leighton (left).
Sputnik (right) was the beginning of the space age.

to Mars. These would carry
instruments to study Mars.

Nearly everyone wanted
a closer look at Mars. The
public wanted to see if
Martians really existed.
Astronomers wanted to
learn more about the red

27

Mariner (left) photographed Mars and its crater Atlantis (right).

planet. Also, there was a
chance that, even if Mars
was dead now, it had had
life in the past.

In 1965 the U.S. probe
Mariner 4 photographed
Mars from a distance of
just 6,100 miles. Those

were the first close-up
pictures of Mars. During
the next 10 years, the
United States and the USSR
launched many other
probes to Mars.

The United States landed
Viking 1 and *Viking 2*
on Mars in 1976. These

Artist's painting shows *Viking* landing on Mars.

The first photos *Viking* took of Mars.

probes tested Mars'
temperature, atmosphere
and soil. People eagerly
studied the thousands of
pictures of Mars' surface
the *Viking* cameras sent
back to Earth.

The probes showed that
the modern astronomers

had been right. Conditions on Mars were too poor to support life. The planet's highest temperatures were about 60°F. But its lowest temperatures fell to -220°F. That is much too cold for human beings. Mars' surface temperature typically is well below 0°F.

Scientists learned that the atmosphere on Mars has very little oxygen. Higher life forms need oxygen to breathe. Mars'

polar caps and some
clouds over the planet
seem to contain frozen
water. But Mars' surface is
so cold it freezes the
water which higher life
forms need.

The probes did not find
canals on Mars, but they
did find out about the
greenish-gray areas. These
areas seem to be sand
and dust that are blown
by the wind at various
times of the Martian year.

Viking photographed these sand dunes.

The pictures sent back
by the probes uncovered
some pleasant surprises.
Mars has more kinds of
scenery than astronomers
had thought. It has many
craters (holes) like those

on the Moon. Most were probably made by meteoroids that struck Mars' surface. (Meteoroids are pieces of stone and metal that race through the Solar System at 40 miles per second.)

The red planet also has canyons up to four miles deep. And it has volcanoes. One huge volcano, Olympus Mons, is about 16 miles tall and about 350 miles across. It is three times as tall as

Olympus Mons is an enormous volcano.

Mount Everest—the Earth's
highest peak.

But the biggest news was
that water may once have
flowed across Mars! The
planet has features that
look like dry riverbeds.

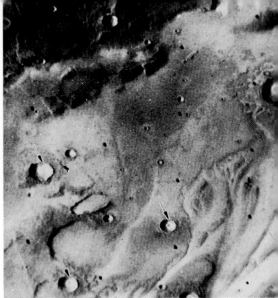

Water flow channel (left) and fog-filled craters (right)

They look like the Earth's
riverbeds would if they
were drained of water.

Some scientists think
these features prove that
Mars once had running water.
If so, the planet was much
warmer than it is today.
Mars may have had the
conditions needed for life.

36

MORE QUESTIONS ABOUT MARS

The news that Mars may once have been more like Earth raised new questions. Did plants and animals once live on Mars? If so, are there fossil remains of those living things?

If Mars was once warmer, and if it had more water, then why did the planet change? Where did the water go? Could

the same thing happen
to the Earth?

No life has been found
on Mars yet. But some
scientists think that Mars
could have tiny living
things beneath its surface.
These life forms could be
so small that they can
be seen only with a
microscope.

More flights to Mars are needed to answer these
and other questions.
People may even have to
visit Mars to answer them.

Mars also is called the red planet

PEOPLE WILL GO TO MARS!

After the *Viking* probes
landed in 1976, the United
States and the USSR did not
launch any Mars missions.
But both nations plan to
explore Mars in the late

1990s. First they will send unmanned probes to study Mars' surface, soil, and weather in great detail.

The USSR has more plans for exploring Mars than the United States has. By 2010, the USSR may even send people to Mars. The United States could send people to Mars a few years later. Perhaps the two nations will work together. In that case people could land on Mars sooner than expected.

The first spaceship may
be launched from a space
station above the Earth.
The trip to Mars will take
a few months. The astronauts
might first go to Phobos,
one of Mars' two little moons.
(The other is Deimos.) From

Phobos

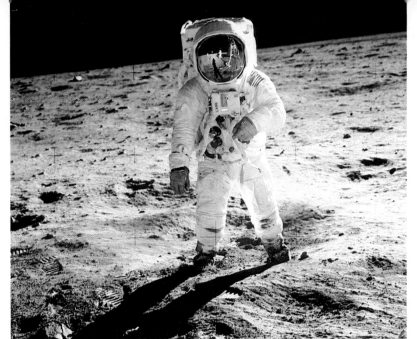

Astronaut Aldrin wore a spacesuit when he explored the moon.

Phobos, the astronauts could travel to Mars.

The astronauts will have to wear spacesuits. The suits will provide them with air and protect them from the cold. The first explorers probably will spend several weeks on Mars.

Mars is much like the Earth in one way. A day on Mars is about 24½ hours long, about the same length as the 24-hour day on the Earth. The 24½ hours is how long Mars takes to spin once.

A year on Mars lasts 687 Earth-days. That is the time the planet takes to orbit the Sun. The Earth's year is 365¼ days—only about half as long as the Martian year.

The astronauts also will

The astronauts are weightless when they travel in space because they are not pulled down by the force of gravity.

find that they weigh less and can jump higher on Mars than they can on the Earth. Because Mars is smaller than the Earth, it has weaker *gravity*. Gravity is the force that pulls things down. A person who weighs 70

pounds on Earth would weigh

Sunset on Mars was photographed by *Viking*.

only 27 pounds on Mars.
The first Mars explorers
may even find proof that
Mars once had life on it.
Perhaps one day you will
be part of the first
expedition to Mars, the red
planet!

FACTS ABOUT MARS

Average Distance from Sun—
About 142 million miles

Closest Approach to Earth—
About 35 million miles

*Diameter—*About 4,200 miles

*Length of Day—*24 hours
and 37 minutes

*Length of Year—*687 Earth-
days

*High Temperatures—*In the
60's F.

*Low Temperatures—*About
-220° F.

*Atmosphere—*Mostly carbon
dioxide, with small amounts
of other gases

*Number of Moons—*2 (Phobos
and Deimos)

*Weight of an Object on Mars
That Would Weigh 100
Pounds on Earth—*38 pounds

*Average Speed as Mars
Orbits the Sun—*About 14½
miles per second

WORDS YOU SHOULD KNOW

astronauts(AST • roh • nawts)—space explorers

astronomers(ah • STRON • ih • merz)—people who study stars,
planets and other heavenly bodies

canals(kuh • NALZ)—ditches built to transport water; it was once
thought that Mars had canals

craters(KRAY • terz)—holes that in many cases were made by
objects from space

Earth(ERTH)—the planet (the 3rd from the Sun) on which we live

flying saucers or UFO's(FLY • ing SAW • serz)—unproven
objects thought by some people to be
alien spacecraft

fossils(FAW • sills)—very old remains of plants and animals

gravity(GRAV • ih • tee)—the force that holds things down to a
heavenly body

Mars(MARZ)—the 4th planet from the Sun

meteoroids(ME • tee • er • oids)—pieces of stone and metal in
the Solar System

microscopes(MIKE • ra • skohpes) — instruments that make very small objects look bigger

million(MILL • yun) — a thousand thousand (1,000,000)

moons(MOONZ) — natural objects that orbit most of the nine planets; Mars has two little moons

orbit(OR • bit) — the path an object takes when it moves around another object

oxygen(OX • ih • jin) — a gas we need to breathe

planets(PLAN • its) — large objects that orbit stars; the Sun has nine planets

Solar System(SO • ler SISS • tim) — the Sun and its "family" of objects

space probes(SPAISS PROHBZ) — unmanned spacecraft sent to study heavenly bodies

space station(SPAISS STAY • shun) — a large man-made satellite on which people can live and work

stars(STARZ) — giant balls of hot, glowing gas

Sun(SUN) — the yellow star that is the closest star to the Earth

telescopes(TEL • ih • skohpz) — instruments that make distant objects look closer

theory(THEER • ee) — idea

volcano(vol • KAY • no) — an opening in the ground through which lava and other material erupt; a mountain, also called a volcano, builds up around the opening

INDEX

air, 22, 42
ancient people, 11, 12, 13
animals, 16, 37
astronauts, 41, 42, 43-44
astronomers, 14, 15, 16, 18-19, 21, 22, 23, 27, 30-31, 33
atmosphere, 30-31, 46
canals, 18, 19-20, 22, 32
canyons, 34
channels, 18
cold, 22, 31, 42
colors, planet, 12-13, 15, 16, 32

craters, 33
day, length of, 43, 46
Deimos, 41, 46
diameter, 46
dust, surface, 32
Earth, 7, 9, 11, 26
Earth-days, 43
exploration, 26-36, 39-45
flying saucers, 24-25
fossils, 37
gods and goddesses, 12, 13
gravity, 44

Herschel, William, 16
ice, 15
invasion, of Earth, 20, 23
Jupiter, 7, 11
life, on Mars, 16-20, 22, 24, 27-28, 31-32, 36, 38
Mariner 4, 28-29
Mars:
    distance from Sun, 7, 11, 13, 17, 46
    similarity to Earth, 17, 43, 44-46

markings on, 15-16, 18
canals on, 19
telescope views of, 22
men from, 25
space probes to, 27, 28-29, 39-45
photographed by *Mariner 4*, 28-29
day's length on, 43
Martians, 17-18, 20, 22, 23-24, 25, 27
Mercury, 6, 11
meteoroids, 34
moons, 8, 41, 46
Mount Everest, 35
Neptune, 7, 11
North Pole, Mars', 15
oceans, 16
Olympus Mons, 34
orbits, 6, 8, 43
oxygen, 31, 36, 37
Phobos, Mars' moon, 41-42, 46
photographs, 28-29, 30, 33
planets, 6-7, 8, 9, 11, 12, 13, 14
plants, 16, 37
Pluto, distance from Sun, 7, 11
polar caps, 15
probes, space, 28, 29-30, 32, 33, 39, 40
red planet, 12-13, 22, 27-28, 34, 36, 45
riverbeds, 35-36
rockets, 26
Romans, 13
sand, 32
satellite, artificial, 26

satellite, first, 26
Saturn, 7, 11
saucers, flying, 24-25
Schiaparelli, Giovanni, 18
scientists, 25, 38
size, star, 5-6
snow, 15
soil tests, 30, 40
Solar System, 5-9, 34
South Pole, Mars, 15
space, 5, 26
spaceships, 24, 41
spring, Mars', 16
Sputnik I, 26
stars, 5-6, 12
summer, Mars', 16
Sun, 5-9
telescopes, 11, 14, 18, 21-25
temperatures, 30-31, 36, 46
time, on Mars, 43
UFOs, (unidentified flying objects), 24
United States, 26, 29, 39, 40
Uranus, 7, 11
Venus, 6, 13
Viking I, 29-30, 39
Viking II, 29-30, 39
volcanoes, on Mars, 34
War of the Worlds, 23
water, 20, 32, 35-36, 37
weather, 40
weight, on Mars, 44, 46
Wells, H. G., 23
wheat fields, 18
wind, on Mars, 32
year, length, 43, 46

About the Author

Dennis Fradin attended Northwestern University on a partial creative scholarship and was graduated in 1967. His previous books include the Young People's Stories of Our States series for Childrens Press, and Bad Luck Tony for Prentice-Hall. In the True book series Dennis has written about astronomy, farming, comets, archaeology, movies, space colonies, the space lab, explorers, and pioneers. He is married and the father of three children.